THINK LIKE AN ARTIST

Connecting To Your Inner Genius

BY
VITAL GERMAINE

Editor: Aim To Win
Cover: Aim To Win
Cover photo: Larry Wong
Interior: Aim To Win

Trade Paperback ISBN: 9798375344447

1. Personal Development
2. Inspiration
3. Creativity

Published by:

AIM TO WIN inc.

Printed in the United States of America

Vital Germaine
Copyright © November 2023 reserved

"A creative life is an amplified life.

It's a bigger life,

a happier life, an expanded life,

and a hell of a lot

more interesting life."

Elizabeth Gilbert

INTRODUCTION

Many wonder by what means pioneers like

Marie Curie, Pablo Picasso, Steve Jobs,

Salvador Dali, Leonardo da Vinci,

Cirque du Soleil director and founder, Franco Dragone,

Guy Laliberté respectively, find the artistic inspiration that

leads to moments of pioneering clarity that

enables them to overcome the seemingly impossible.

Where do they find the courage, ideas and resilience

to disrupt and continue their creative paths

when the world is telling them no.

Can anybody sign up?

Yes, anybody can sign up and tap

into that original source.

We are all gifted with creative potential.

It's a question of how to channel and

leverage that potential for a richer life,

both at home and at work.

THINK LIKE AN ARTIST is about

connecting to the power of your creativity.

The business/leadership equivalent

of this book is titled,

INNOVATION MINDSET.

People often confuse art with creativity.

They overlap but are

significantly different.

Not everybody is an artist.

However…

EVERYBODY IS CREATIVE.

NOT EVERYBODY IS A CREATIVE.

Furthermore, art is a skill or talent.

Whereas creativity is a MINDSET.

I Ieverage both qualities when in my art studio.

As an entrepreneur / keynote speaker, I leverage

only creativity while thinking like an artist...

an artist who creates and designs not only the

work, but also the journey from ideation to completion.

I am using Cirque du Soleil as a

case study I lived for over

5 years and 2 thousand shows.

Their journey from obscurity to global recognition is one

based on combining business creativity with pure art.

Let's explore and discover the magic.

CHAPTER 1

NOW WAY

Every now and again,

something happens in life that outshines

everything else: an aha moment,

or a dream you've worked on for years,

suddenly comes to fruition.

Perhaps it's the realization

you've met your soul mate

at a glance, or a door you've

been knocking on for years

finally opens.

There are endless

significant events that can

potentially propel us

into a completely different

and life-changing direction.

I'd like to share a singular creative

moment that arguably changed the

trajectory of Cirque du Soleil.

There was

Cirque

before

this moment,

and Cirque after

this moment.

CHAPTER 2

SANTA'S MASSIVE SUPRISE

The highly anticipated premiere of

Cirque du Soleil's first permanent

Show, *Mystère*, would unfold on

December 25, 1993.

That Christmas Eve was

one of those unforgettable

and defining days.

What a priceless lesson on how

to seize a moment, spread your wings,

reach higher and become more than

who or what you were.

This occurrence set me on a

path to think differently,

dream bigger and achieve more.

That Christmas Eve morning,

we began our final rehearsal of

Mystère set to open the next day,

December 25th –

Santa had a massive surprise up his sleeve.

We had been training, practicing,

and rehearsing or onboarding if

you will, for almost a year,

with most of that time spent in

Montreal, Cirque's HQ.

During that final rehearsal

one of the performers

did something unexpected in the

teeter-board act...

the teeter board is like a huge

seesaw, where acrobats

bounce up and down, fly,

do multiple flips and land on

shoulders and other crazy,

dangerous death-defying stuff.

What that acrobat did

was totally out of context.

It caught the attention of the director,

Franco Dragone from Belgium.

It must have ignited a spark in him.

As a result, Franco said something

in his thick Belgian, French accent.

He said passionately to the acrobat,

"I like zis verrrghy verrrghy much."

Pointed at that acrobat and said,

"Show me zis again."

Now, we'd heard this phrase,

show me zis again,

for almost a year.

If he liked what he saw, he'd say,

"Everrrghybody do like zis."

And we all did like zis.

Rehearsal would continue as

he built or experimented with

that suggestion. However,

that Christmas Eve rehearsal

was very different.

What he said next was something

we'd never heard before.

There was Cirque du Soleil,

before this moment,

and Cirque du Soleil

after this moment.

After saying,

"Everrrghybody, do like zis,'

he said something that

blew our minds.

He said…

CHAPTER 3

WHEN IT ALL GOES TERRIBLY WRONG. THEN WHAT?

Before revealing what Franco

said, what does one do

when life places a gigantic hurdle

in front of you or knocks

you down? Because it will

at some point. It is our

imagination or creativity that provides

all answers and solutions.

It is the artist within you that

will adapt and leverage

its imagination to problem-solve.

That's what artists do.

They continually problem-solve

because they are regularly

"failing".

Be curious,

Be childlike and have courage.

Learn how

to leverage your imagination

and overcome everything

and anything life throws at you.

Fly beyond the net and

be free to live your fullest life.

The artist has freed themselves from

the net and conformity. It's a very scary, yet

highly empowering mindset.

In many ways, the artist

connects to their emotions and their inner child.

The healthy untainted, uncorrupt inner child

is the human superpower. Children are compelled

by their yet untethered imagination

fueled by what they feel, think, see, taste and hear.

Add spontaneity and they find

themselves absorbed in the moment.

During the artistic process, boundaries,

ceilings and limiting beliefs disappear.

Why?

Because during creation, the artist is

often caught up **in the moment**.

Caught up in pure childlike wonderment,

curiosity, and exploration.

When you are truly in the moment,

there is no thought.

Life simply happens.

Creativity happens.

Your inner genius comes through

in alignment with purpose and intention.

Vincent van Gogh once said,

"The emotions are sometimes so strong

that I work without knowing it.

The strokes come like speech."

Wheeeeee!

IF YOU ASK ME WHAT I CAME TO DO IN THIS WORLD, I, AN ARTIST, WILL ANSWER YOU: I AM HERE TO LIVE OUT LOUD.

— ÉMILE ZOLA.

CHAPTER 4

LAUNCHING PAD

Curiosity leads to exploration.

Exploration leads to discovery.

Discovery leads to solutions.

Dare to dream!

The inner child is filled

with dreams.

It is adults who stifle the

dreams and infinite possibility

of children with their fear-driven no's.

"Don't do this.

Don't do that.

Get down from there.

Stop.

No, no, no, no, no!"

Children hear 232 no's a day on average.

At each no, their inner genius

is starved of the freedom to

BE.

Dare to dream BIG.

Dream so big it scares you.

Then let your imagination run wild

about all the great things that

might happen. Besides…

The world needs the curious

creatives and artists.

They are the ones

who change the world …

inspire progress and innovation.

They are the ones who dare

to dream, who dare to do,

and who dare to become.

We all have this mindset or

superpower within us.

Consider the mind as a

muscle that can be stimulated

and trained to grow and become

bigger, better, faster, and stronger.

It's a magical tool that can

unlock all and any doors.

Everybody is creative

Not everybody is **a** creative.

Like all tools, they can and

should be sharpened, shined,

and well-maintained. You never know

when you're going to need it.

That journey begins in the imagination.

Albert Einstein once said,

"Logic will take you from A to B.

Imagination will take you everywhere."

CREATIVITY IS NEITHER

A SKILL NOR A TALENT.

IT'S A MINDSET.

CHAPTER 5

OPPORTUNITY

So much opportunity awaits on the

other side of a closed door.

The blank canvas can be viewed as

an overwhelming door.

Where and how do I open it or

begin the journey?

That's what I mean by mindset.

You determine if it's an

opportunity or a threat.

The artist sees a blank canvas

and jumps for joy at the opportunity

of creating something… anything.

Unless writer's block has cuckold them.

Have confidence and

optimism to open that door

and curiously peek.

That's what artists do. We peek.

We explore. We take risks.

We discover and grow.

We fail... who cares.

We erase.

We start again until the

work of art presents itself... sometimes

hours, days, weeks later... but it appears.

We know it's a constant work in progress.

This relieves some pressure.

We are learning. We are growing.

We are becoming.

Just keep your mind open...

open to possibility.

A MIND IS LIKE A PARACHUTE.

IT DOESN'T WORK IF IT' IS NOT OPEN.

FRANK ZAPPA

CHAPTER 6

RISK AND ADAPTABILITY

The daring of Cirque and Franco!

All it took to change the trajectory

of an organization and endless

individuals connected to it,

was one bold, daring, inspirational

flash of inventive genius from a director.

This single act defined and embodied

every aspect of empowerment that the word

"creativity" encompasses.

This event, which I'm excited

to share, recalibrated the

trajectory of the now most

famous and innovative

modern circus of our generation.

Le Cirque du Soleil.

The visionary idea of *Mystère*

director, Franco Dragone,

that ignited this mammoth

change was more daring than

any death-defying, fire-juggling

act I'd ever seen.

Millions of investor dollars

and reputations could disappear

in a plume of smoke if his

last-gasp idea failed.

Chapter 7

MAGICAL PROCESS

Cirque's formation has parallels

to growing up.

Parents, teachers and the likes,

inform, inspire, train and groom

us along our tour of life.

In adulthood and when entering

the "real" world of work and

entrepreneurship, it's called

onboarding, or figuring that stuff

out as you go along. It's an attitude.

It's a mindset, which is in big part

driven by our beliefs, expectations,

choices and habits; AKA,

your character.

Choose your values well for

they define who you become.

They are your foundation,

your launching pad to fly

and reach higher.

I mean... they even adopted

and transformed an abandoned

fire station in Montreal,

affectionately named Angus,

to become their "factory".

There was no avant-garde

interior design on display.

There were no Oompa Loompas

meandering the premises doing

strange dances.

Nonetheless...

… the fact they had chosen

an abandoned fire station sent

a subliminal message that

they were cool, fun, eccentric,

and defying context —

open-minded and open to

exploration and discovery.

I couldn't wait to start.

Wheeeeee!

The air and behavior inside

Angus reeked of dedication,

focus, advancement, passion,

and a commitment to excellence.

"Reach Higher," echoed from each nook,

cranny and crevice.

Most performers were

former Olympians, award winning

acrobats, jugglers, dancers,

and actors from around the world.

Myself, and several others,

were hired for our potential

that was magnified by our attitude:

an attitude of, "Why not?

Yes, I will try that because

everything has potential."

Trying the new and the

not before seen is Cirque's

default setting.

Experiment, fail, learn, grow,

and discover is written on

their walls in invisible ink.

The words can't be read,

only **felt** and brought to

life through doing,

trying, and falling.

Franco continually reinforced

that mentality in his approach.

I soaked it up and became

more courageous in my personal endeavors.

We always obeyed and did "like zis"

even though we sometimes

feared and doubted.

Fear and doubt are the

biggest enemies of

growth, sustainability

relevance.

This final day of rehearsal was

no different, despite the premier

waiting just hours away beyond the wings.

Franco pointed at Travis;

a short compact American

acrobat who had unknowingly

done something inspirational.

"I like zis verrrghy verrrghy much,"

Franco declared. "Show me zis again."

The reward of having our idea,

seen, heard and experimented with,

inspired, fulfilled, and engaged us.

It personified the spirit of contribution, collaboration,

and appreciation —

Travis obliged and repeated his move.

"Magnifique. Give me more pride."

Travis raised his chin.

"Oui. Now, more muscle in *ze* arm.

Chest big. Chin even higher,

like you are ze prince of Vegas."

Travis clenched his fists and

extended his neck.

His exposed shoulder muscles bulged.

The veins in his forearms tripled in size.

"What can you do to 'aving more power?"

added Franco, his eyes impatiently

fixed on the response.

A brief pause punctuated the mood.

Travis jumped in the air like a

superhero blocking a Dr. Evil "laser"

attack to planet Earth with his shaved pecs.

"Oui! Yes, Travis! Jump again.

Only one leg… more…

continue stepping in ze air

one leg after ze other."

We watched, wanting to be the next

to add our unique color to

this optimistic adventure.

Travis' robust and elegant

strides powered him around the

large psychedelic blue and green stage.

The theatre became quiet,

disturbed only by the intense

concentration of the genius

director at work and Travis leaping

around like an alien-like gazelle.

Travis' energy and muscle tension

waned a little from doing several laps.

He looked at Franco for permission to stop.

Franco gestured to continue,

passion leaving his fingertips like

lightning bolts from Thor's hammer.

We were nearly always

pushed to take that extra step,

to add an additional color

and offer one more possibility,

one more option.

That extra suggestion might be

THE defining one.

"Merci."

Travis gasped for air in relief

as he came to a quick and needed halt.

Franco walked around the stage

eying us all.

His deep, introspective dark eyes

pierced the silence.

We waited.

Sometimes his response

was immediate and void

of analysis; other times,

I could see the tautness of

the cogs and pulleys twisting

and turning in his brain.

Would his metaphoric thumb

condemn Travis with a downward

motion, or would the American

gymnast live another day to

try something new and

increase his contribution.

Franco stood in silence…

"Everrrghybody, do like *zis!"*

Two thumbs up and a jeer

from the coliseum crowd.

His mix of French (*francais*)

and English (*anglais*),

combined to create, Franglais

(as we call it in French) was entertaining.

We all watched in wonderment

and fear as nonsensical images

morphed into rhyme, noise became music,

chaos turned into choreography,

and ordinary performers transformed

into extraordinary beings with

wings and almost superhuman powers.

I wondered what could happen

if I implemented a little bit of

Cirque du Soleil and Franco Dragone

into my life.

How much higher could I reach?

How much higher could you reach?

ART WASHES AWAY FROM THE SOUL
THE DUST OF EVERYDAY LIFE.

- PABLO PICASSO

CHAPTER 8

HOW I GOT INTO CIRQUE

I auditioned for Cirque

while living in Manhattan…

a typical starving artist,

living in a rat-infested studio

on 108th Street, Spanish Harlem.

Endless rejections at previous

auditions had led me to believe

my dream was a stupid endeavor.

I should have listened to all

the naysayers back home in Belgium,

who suggested I get a "simple" job

like everybody else in the town.

"You'll never make it in New York.

What are you thinking, Vital?

You're wasting your time

but go ahead and be stubborn.

You'll see."

Ever heard this or something

similar from your "friends?"

Artists tend to not listen to naysayers.

We live with conviction and passion

for our expression and path.

Are you living with conviction and passion

for your authentic path?

If not passion, conviction and discipline

to get you there.

Some people don't and can't

understand when something compels you.

They are oblivious to that deep

yearning to pursue the ridiculous.

Many feel too at home in the safety of

their comfort zone, reluctant to

risk, fail, learn, discover, and progress.

If it works for you, I have no issues.

Each must live life according

to their needs, values,

expectations and desires.

I'm inviting you to become more.

I'm daring you to reach higher.

There is no one-size-fits-all formula in life.

I simply encourage people to take

that risk, discover and grow.

Listen to your inner voice, your inner child,

your calling, your purpose.

It belongs to nobody else.

Once you've identified your calling or purpose,

protect it and go for it.

Full out!

Embrace the perils and the soreness.

It's cliché, but the magic really

does happen out of your

comfort zone and when

you trust the process...

and yourself.

CHAPTER 9

THE DREADFUL COMFORT ZONE

YOU ARE HERE

ALL CHANGE,
GROWTH AND
TRANSFORMATION
HAPPENS HERE

COMFORT
ZONE

ZONE OF GENIUS

PANIC ZONE !

The Cirque du Soleil audition

was down at Battery Park.

Walking lost in the park

I stumbled upon a big yellow-and-blue

tent that dwarfed the trees.

It stood wrapped in a mysterious stillness —

deserted almost.

Only a cool breeze blowing from the

Hudson River accompanied

its strange solitude.

The casting director, Nicolette,

greeted and guided me into

the belly of the tent.

The Big Top appeared familiar and weird.

I had been to Barnum & Bailey before,

but where was the customary

stench of elephant dung

and horse sweat?

I imagined the ringmaster snapping

his whip to alert the lions,

even though animals in cages

always troubled me.

I wondered where they hid the human cannon.

Where's the sawdust?

I hadn't a clue.

One of the other auditioning

performers mentioned that

this weird circus from

Montreal didn't use animals.

No animals.

That's not a circus...

That's silly!

To read about the entire

Cirque du Soleil audition,

I invited you to read my book,

FLYING WITHOUT A NET 2.0

CHAPTER 10

THE CONVICTION OF A LEFT HOOK

Creativity, authenticity and

freedom of expression takes

bravery, nerve, mettle,

and sprinkles of audacity to

fight off the protectors of tradition.

Disruption requires courage.

It necessitates a conviction to

left-hook the doubters in the face,

and fight off the skeptics with

pepper spray before they violate

your creativity or your dream.

I could have never imagined

that a moment of pure freedom

and naiveté for a silly "unknown"

circus without animals would

pave the way to my American Dream.

What's in the way of you and your dream?

Is it YOU?

I found myself at the heart of

Cirque's stage, transforming

into a vastly improved

version of myself.

Creativity is a

not a skill

or a talent.

It's a mindset.

It's also a physical thing

in the

sense that you

can train your brain

to literally reconfigure itself

and fire differently;

synapses.

Synapses connect neurons

in the brain to other neurons.

The artist has an ability to

allow new synapses to develop

through exploration and experimentation.

This approach to life, minimizes

cognitive dissonance.

CHAPTER 11

CHALLENGES

In this chapter I am

setting you a series of physical

and mental challenges that

will help you stimulate new

synapse in your brain

and minimize Cognitive Dissonance:

having inconsistent thoughts, ideals, values etc.

that prevent us from living authentically and freely

due to fear or confusion. It incites fear, making us

cling to certain behaviors rather than embrace

that which is different.

These simple activities can be

done in your own time,

whenever you like.

Please revisit this chapter regularly

for reminders that will

continually help you

grow and reach higher.

This mindset of continual growth

is called KAIZEN

in Japanese.

1.

To inspire new synapses to fire,

enabling your creativity to grow

and expand your mind, I am

challenging you to handwrite your

name 10 times with the other hand.

So, if you are left-handed, attempt the

challenge with your right hand.

2.

I am challenging you to drive or

walk anywhere familiar via a

different route. Pay attention to

the new colors, sounds and emotions.

3.

I am challenging you to

brush your teeth with your

other hand for just 2 days.

4.

This one you will need to do in real time.

I am challenging you to cross your arms.

Which arm/hand is on top?

Now, without thinking, quickly open your

arms then recross them, but this time with the

opposite arm/hand on top.

If you feel or experience any sense of awkwardness

or clumsiness in crossing your arms differently,

it's normal. It's due to the synapses in your brain

trying to find the familiar pattern. A new pattern

forces the brain to create new synapses. This

feels uncomfortable. Through training your brain

to be ok with the uncomfortable, you develop resilience.

Resilience leads to elevated self-confidence.

By stepping regularly out of your comfort

zone and teaching the brain that new and different

is okay, you are minimizing the paralyzing

impact of Cognitive Dissonance.

We experience Cognitive Dissonance as well

whenever our beliefs (religious, political etc.), core

values or life experiences are challenged.

Creativity opens the mind.

CHAPTER 12

CREATIVE MINDSET

The growth mindset or creative

spirit impacts society on all levels,

ranging from business to sports

and our personal lives.

Having a growth mindset is only

the beginning of the creative process.

Cirque du Soleil started from a

strong forward-thinking mindset,

yet didn't thrive from day one.

They continually experimented,

learned and **adapted** in all they did. In the book,

Origin of the Species, Charles Darwin said,

"It's not the strongest or most intelligent

of the species that survives but the one

that's the most adaptable

to change".

Bruce Lee understood this concept

with great depth. He once said,

"Be Water, My Friend.

Empty your mind.

Be formless, shapeless, like water.

You put water into a cup, it becomes the cup.

You put water into a bottle, it becomes the bottle.

You put it into a teapot, it becomes the teapot.

Now, water can flow or it can crash.

Be water, my friend."

How well you adapt will be heavily

influenced by your environment and

those in your circle.

Cirque made a point to have access

to a pool of incredible people

who heavily impacted

the creative process.

Who's in your pool or circle

that will elevate your worth

and contribute to your

entrepreneurial venture

or personal world?

Be strategic regarding who you

trust and bring into your life.

They will heavily impact

your ability to imagine

a bright and hopeful

tomorrow based on

their influence on

your mindset... your

CREATIVITY!

CHAPTER 13

HEALING & RESILIENCE

It takes great pain, suffering and tragedy

to create the most amazing art.

Alongside that, expression through art is

one of the most therapeutic and healing

activities a human can do.

Through creativity we heal.

Through healing we gain self-confidence

and develop resilience.

This does not mean I'm expecting

you to become an artist.

I invite you to be more creative.

I invite you to be free to express.

I invite you to release your emotions,

experiences and thoughts.

If it's not for healing, then let it be

for self-confidence and resilience.

The tragedy of the tortured artist is

being overwhelmed with emotion.

Emotions need to fly free.

But releasing them into the world

is scary AF!

What will people think?

What about my FIMAGE (fear of image).

Here is the magical safety net of art.

One can express themselves, revealing

the darkest of shadows, the most

regretful and weak moments through

music, painting, theatre...

the list of ways to express is long.

With all that vulnerability, feeling naked

and exposed, the artist is protected!

How?

Because, until you reveal the exact story

or meaning behind your expression,

people don't know if it's something

YOU are, or have experienced,

or if it's something you've seen and

are telling the story of another person.

This same principal applies

with general story-telling.

In Cirque, I would and could express an

array of emotions during the show.

One day I expressed romantic love.

The next day I was pissed off at company

policy and one or two assholes in the cast.

That same day, but in the second show

perhaps I was emotionally, spiritually,

mentally and physically exhausted…

I expressed determination.

Some days, my heart was bleeding.

I cried stoic tears of salvation,

Knowing this too shall pass.

That's empowering wisdom right "therrr",

In everyday life, we can all express ourselves.

It doesn't have to be through art,

but artistic expression goes deep into the

belly of one's soul.

One must be alone and see one's emotional

reflection to truly know what they are feeling,

desiring, fearing, expecting.

Arts and crafts are meditative, too.

Cooking. The clothes you choose.

The color and style of your hair.

There are endless ways to express,

vent and release, and nobody will be

the wiser because you are protected through

the metaphorical and theatrical "fourth wall"

that separates the artist from the audience and reality.

The fourth wall is magical and powerful...

and you can create it.

Art is therapy. As a bonus, releasing

pent-up anger, or frustration on a canvas

(or other creative channel)

is much healthier than taking it

out on people you love.

I discovered painting by accident.

Or painting discovered me. Then

I became very intentional with it.

Either way, it has saved me and

empowered me in many ways.

I'm confident that thinking

like an artist and doing something

artistic will liberate and empower you, too.

CHAPTER 14

REMINDER

Creativity is an organic process

that must be experimented

with and set free, even

when misunderstood and scary.

One seemingly wrong or

bad idea becomes a good idea.

With revisions and prototyping,

that idea has now become a better idea.

Which then changes into a great idea,

Eventually transforms into the right idea.

The process repeats at each idea,

knowing there is no guarantee

of the outcome.

It's a question of allowing an

original idea or goal to breathe and

grow before murdering it at its birth.

It's parallel to the process of a painter

standing in front of a blank canvas.

It can be stressful or exciting.

Both perspectives trigger very

similar emotional and

physical reactions: increased heart rate,

elevated blood pressure. Perhaps even sweaty palms.

It all depends how you package the situation.

#mindset

CHANGE IS INEVITABLE.

TRANSFORMATION IS A CHOICE.

Change is never easy to

embrace or initiate.

Most are afraid of the new, the different,

and the unknown.

Celebrated Canadian writer and

motivational speaker Robin Sharma says,

"Change is hard at first.

Messy in the middle.

Gorgeous at the end."

I was often afraid

during Cirque's process.

Afraid to step so far out of

my comfort zone.

Afraid to fail or disappoint.

Afraid I wasn't good enough to

travel this optimistic journey

with an amazing company

that expected nothing

less than extraordinary.

Get over your fear.

Fear is the number one

killer of dreams.

Most of the cast **resisted** the

Cirque process at first.

We resist what we don't

understand or what scares us.

Fear can paralyze.

It can also be a very powerful motivator.

The key to failing is to fail quickly.

Nelson Mandela once said,

"I never lose, I either win or I learn."

Once we learned, as a cast,

to embrace this different approach

and become more open-minded,

adventurous, and unattached

to the outcome,

we became empowered.

We grew wings and reached so much

higher than we thought we could or would.

We discovered so much more

about our limits and ourselves.

The ceiling disappeared

into the abyss of the proverbial box.

It made us better.

Set us free.

The ultimate mindset of the artist

is freedom to be. Freedom to express.

Freedom from what others think because

we are simply doing our thang!

I wonder what real life would be

like to live with such freedom of

childlike exploration, risk, learning,

adaptation, and discovery void of a

box or limiting beliefs.

At the end of Franco's barrage of

creative challenges and

relentless "show me zis again,"

and "Everrrghybody do like zis,"

we experienced a new and

never-before voiced request from him.

It blew our minds.

And this is all at the eleventh hour.

The premiere was the next day!

He said...

"Forgghhget everyyyghssing you 'ave learn.

We start all over wiz zis new energy."

Is he for real?

Chapter 15

STAY CALM AND CARRY ON

We panicked.

His famous words changed the

direction of the teeterboard act

and the trajectory of what is now

the most renowned modern

circus of our generation.

Their future might have not been so

glamorous and lucrative had he

not acted on his artistic

genius and courage.

Yes, he really did say,

"Forgghhget everyyyghssing you 'ave learn.

We start all over wiz zis new energy."

After almost a year of formation

and rehearsal, you want us to

"forgghhget everyyyghssing

you 'ave learn."

The teeterboard performers

stopped in their tracks and

looked at each other for verification

that they had all heard the same request.

Seated in the obscurity of the empty

theatre seats, I gasped,

eyebrows raised to code red levels.

Cirque had pushed us beyond

push and challenged us beyond challenge.

This might have been a bridge too far.

In moments of great challenge

and adversity we must dig

deepest lest the imagination take

a southerly direction inviting worry,

stress, and emotional paralysis.

I'm not going to have a job!

My American dream would end

before it even started.

I had no desire to return to the struggles of

Manhattan life in a rat-infested studio

in Spanish Harlem.

I fought so hard and overcame

so much. As had Cirque and

their pioneering founders.

Hours of apprehension snaked

through the cast's collective psyche

as we waited and waited.

We felt like abandoned toddlers.

Nobody to spoon-feed or burp us.

Nobody to share the plan and

the anticipated outcome.

Nothing but concern,

worry, and stress.

Negative gossip spread like

determined fire ants invading

a rival colony. American engineer

and inventor of the modern air conditioner,

Willis Carrier, suggests we ask this question

in times of stress:

"What's the worst thing that

could happen?"

The worst-case scenario rarely happens.

If it does, it's probably out

of our control. If it's out of our control,

then why worry, I guess?

Stoicism has its place and time.

The fortunate, or smart, performers

relaxed, slept, and didn't worry.

Humans are resilient,

in particular, when they pull together.

"Places, please!"

The bigger the risk,

the bigger the reward.

Dig deep, take a deep breath

and go for it.

Trust that your wings will

emerge before you hit the ground.

Scary stuff when we might literally

smash into the ground and

end our careers, lest die from a fall!

Trust and believe anyway.

Chapter 16

BONKERS OR BANANAS

"Forgghhget everyyyghssing you 'ave learn,

we start all over wiz zis new energy."

Franco, you are a nut!

His words would test more than

just our resolve as performers.

This is one day before the premiere,

at the end of almost a year of formation

and rehearsal, and you want us to

'forchget everyssing you 'ave learn,

we start all over wiz zis new energy.'

Franco's words tested more than
just our resolve as performers.
Every single staff member in the company,
ranging from carpenters to rigging,
automation, production and marketing,
to executive management in the
Montreal headquarters, to then
Treasure Island Hotel owner Steve Wynn,
his board members and investors,
would all have to buy into this
theatrical and business insanity.

Change the wardrobe immediately

to accommodate this

"new-found energy"!

The fat-bellied, blue and white

Spermato costumes that had

been practiced in for months

would no longer work. Different music.

New tricks.

Altered choreography.

That change affected the

statement of *Mystère* and

probably saved the show that

up until then lacked. Steve Wynn

had apparently wanted to

shut us down or delay the opening

because the show was too dark,

too slow.

Mr. Wynn and his then wife, Elaine,

had watched the show days

before and were apparently not

impressed, we had been told. *Mystère*,

"the flower in the desert,"

was boring, they had allegedly said.

This last rehearsal day ended up

being the longest I've ever been a

part of in any capacity

of my entire entertainment carrier.

Like most performers,

I've clocked some rehearsal

hours over the years.

We started at ten in the morning,

worked until four the next morning,

went home, ate, and tried to sleep

for a couple of hours.

Some stayed and slept in the theater

because they were too tired

to drive home.

Four hours later, at eight the

same morning, we were back

on stage in costume ready to

rehearse some more.

This is where professionalism,

discipline, dedication, focus,

emotional and mental stamina,

and commitment come into play.

They are all crucial character

traits for those who wish to succeed.

If you are filled with passion,

then discipline and the other

traits almost happen by default.

If you don't have passion, you'd

better have plenty of discipline.

Be passionate!

The premiere was in less

than twelve hours.

Circumstance and lack of time

dictated that we were never

granted the opportunity to

adapt all parts of the show.

The shot clock had run out.

We'd have to perform the

premiere without ever actually

having run the show beginning to end.

"And now, *Mesdames et Messieurs,*

for my next Vegas magic trick…

I am going to pull a miracle

out of my ass."

CHAPTER 17

LAUNCH PAD

Creativity is freedom.

It helps us design a better life

for ourselves by allowing us to

envision and apply solutions

that negate roadblocks and

defy locked doors.

It helps us quell our demons,

conquer our limiting beliefs,

and provide options.

It helps us heal from our past wounds,

in particular, childhood trauma.

But what exactly is creativity,

and how do we leverage its power?

Creativity, like imagination,

is very hard to define.

The fundamental difference

between the two is that imagination

requires no intent or action.

Creativity is the implementation

of what the imagination reveals.

Creativity offers an outcome

based on a strategy that can

be calculated, spontaneous, conceptual,

abstract, and unscripted.

It needs action or expression

in order to have any significant value.

Common thought associates

creativity with art.

This misconception in meaning intimidates.

It leads people to believe

they are not creative.

There is nothing further from the truth.

Everybody is creative and

has the ability to envision,

adapt, and design better lives for themselves.

This doesn't mean that we

are all equally creative.

Like everything in life, ability is relative.

Natural aptitude means you start

in a better pole position, though

the level of effort made to develop

potential is what differentiates

between the average and the extraordinary.

We are all born creative geniuses.

When people claim to not be creative,

what they really mean is that

they are not artistic.

Yes, heightened creativity

and a few other components

do indeed lead to art,

but creativity is not limited to

art as an outcome.

The masses get sucked into this misconception.

The fallacy derives from

how we're taught 'creativity' at school.

We are given colored pencils

and crayons in class,

hence the association with art.

As a result, people often convince

themselves that they are not

creative because they weren't

good at drawing or coloring at school.

This limiting belief breeds insecurity

in one's adult potential.

This absence of confidence

confines people to the safety of their

comfort zone —

a zone that invites personal stagnation,

professional disengagement,

and business irrelevance.

The good news again is

"everybody is creative!"

Even those of you

who think you're not.

EVERYBODY IS CREATIVE.

NOT EVERYBODY IS **A** CREATIVE.

CHAPTER 18

TEN BEHAVOIRS TO ENHANCE CREATIVITY

1. SPEND TIME ALONE - SOLITUDE

2. TAKE TIME TO DO NOTHING

3. BE CURIOUS

4. ALLOW YOUR THOUGHTS TO ROAM FREE

5. READ FICTION, PLAY GAMES, LISTEN TO MUSIC (CLASSICAL AND NEW AGE)

6. DEFY CONFORMITY

7. NEGATE REASONING AND LOGIC

8. CONNECT WITH YOUR INNER CHILD

9. DAYDREAM

10. EXPRESS AND SHARE IDEAS

P.S. You'll find many of your ideas will come while you are in the shower or out walking. So, go for lots of walks… (and take many showers).

CHAPTER 19

ORIGINS OF CREATIVITY

Elizabeth Gilbert, author of

Eat Pray Love, shares her wisdom

in an interesting TED talk titled

"Your Elusive Creative Genius."

She shares how the Ancient Greeks

believed that creativity did not

come from humans.

Creativity originates from

"a divine attendant spirit that came

to human beings from some distant

unknowable source for distant

and unknowable reasons."

She adds that these divine

sources were called "daemons."

The Ancient Romans

called that creative disembodied spirit

"genius."

Genius is a voice that lives

in the walls of one's

studio or workspace.

This theory does more than

give ownership of creativity

to a higher power.

It also protects the earthly

creator of that work from

narcissism and critique.

If the work is so great, the

architect can't take the credit.

If the work is terrible,

they don't get blamed

because it means that their

daemon is lame.

This divine premise changed

drastically at the time of the

Renaissance when the human

being was placed at the center

of the universe.

The result of this intellectual

paradigm shift is that people

now perceived and believed

that creativity came from an

individual, the self.

Instead of

"having a genius"

as the Greeks viewed it,

people now "are the genius."

CHAPTER 20

3-STEP PROCESS

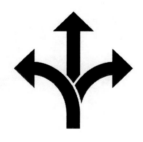

THERE ARE 3 SIMPLE STEPS TO STIMULATING YOUR CREATIVITY.

1. AWARENESS.

Be aware of the genius that sleeps within you.

Your inner Da Vinci is patiently

waiting for you to tap into its frequency.

Awareness comes in two parts.

A. Self-Awareness:

Know who you are; be conscious

of what you do, how and

why you do it. Connect to your values.

Be very aware of your senses.

Don't just look. See!

Don't just hear the noise.

Listen to the sounds.

Dissect and understand

the sounds — the nuances,

the subtleties.

Take the time to break down

what you taste

when eating and drinking.

Allow your brain to register the

textures of things you touch

or that touch you and so forth.

Self-awareness overlaps into

the realm of mindfulness.

How well do you know

yourself? What are your

deal breakers? Where do

you set boundaries?

Maybe the most important aspect

of self-awareness is knowing

your Core Values!

**Core Values: Fundamental beliefs and highest
priorities that drive their behavior.**

On the next page you will find a list

of the top 30 recurring core values.

Review them and eliminate 10 of them.

You should have 20 left over.

Write those 20 on a digital

or hard copy note pad.

1. Efficiency

2. Balance

3. Fairness

4. Creativity

5. Hard Work

6. Learning

7. Competence

8. Compassion

9. Community

10. Security

11. Loyalty

12. Status

13. Charity

14. Teamwork

15. Friendship

16. Adventure

17. Freedom

18. Boldness

19. Success

20. Authority

21. Recognition

22. Spirituality

23. Humility

24. Diversity

25. Humor

26. Kindness

27. Optimism

28. Empathy

29. Fun

30. Accountability

Take those 20 Core Values you

selected and narrow

them down to 10!

Write those 10 on a digital

or hard copy note pad.

But wait!

There's more.

Look carefully at your

list of 10 Core Values.

Do they define you?

Do you live by them?

If so, congrats.

If not, it could mean

you are not living authentically.

Adjust accordingly.

But wait!

There's still more.

Take those 10 Core Values you

selected and narrow

them down to only 4!

Yes, only 4.

A tip to help you narrow them

down to only 4.

You will find that some

Values overlap.

For example,

compassion and empathy

are very similar, so

one could be eliminated.

Same with charity and community.

Write those 4 on a digital

or hard copy note pad.

Even better, frame them.

That's the essence of who you are!

Live by them. They define

your character or personal brand.

Know thyself.

B. External Awareness:

Be aware of your surroundings,

people, and environment.

The more you observe and

pay attention to life

and absorb that information,

the more information you

have stored in your library

of resources or knowledge to

use as inspiration

at a later time.

2. Emotions

Acknowledging your emotions

and allow yourself to feel.

Despite being similar and connected,

emotions and feelings are

different from each other.

The simple version is that emotions

are triggered in the subcortical

regions of the brain,

like the amygdala.

Emotions stimulate chemical

reactions that alter our physical state.

Feelings are the brain's reactions

or interpretations of those

chemicals (emotions).

Beliefs and memories will

impact our feelings.

Everything we do in life is based on what or

how we feel — our emotions.

The more you allow yourself to feel,

the stronger the desire will

be to either quell the pain,

or to add fuel to the pleasure.

Love and hate are the two

strongest emotions that

motivate action.

We are born with love,

but we learn hate.

Embrace emotions.

Allow yourself to feel.

Dare to be vulnerable.

Become more creative

as a result.

Acknowledge and understand

your own emotions.

Our feelings motivate us

to act and find solutions that

improve our lives.

Utilize your pain. Optimize your joy.

The more intense the emotion,

the stronger the odds of action.

The caveat here is that

sometimes our emotional response

is linked to the wrong issue.

Take time to correctly identify

the true emotion or need and,

therefore, the true problem.

What do I mean by the true problem?

We sometimes focus on

something we desire,

believing in our desire.

However, if we analyze and

evaluate that desire more closely

and break it down,

we discover that the true desire

is not what we first thought.

Don't be caged in by

limited perception of possibility

by focusing on the wrong

need or problem.

Dig deeper.

WHEN YOU'RE HAPPY, YOU ENJOY THE
MUSIC BUT WHEN YOU'RE SAD, YOU
UNDERSTAND THE LYRICS.

- FRANK OCEAN

3. Expression Of Our Feelings Into Action.

We must take action

or express ourselves

with meaning — ingenuity.

Ingenuity is the act of being clever

for the application of new ideas.

Without application, ideas collect

dust and decay, dying from inertia.

Ideas don't need a completed strategy.

Often, it's a question of

starting and building momentum.

Through action, ideas morph,

and lead to new ideas.

It can sometimes invite

frustration and doubt.

Struggle is good!

Re-valuation too is good.

The best fuel for ideas is to

have fun with them as they grow.

Einstein said:

"Imagination is intelligence having fun."

When we are having FUN,

we tend to open up and free ourselves.

When we're having fun, we tend to be

less inhibited, we become more receptive

to change, we are filled with enthusiasm.

Inspiration finds us more easily when

we're having fun. Joy energizes and

motivates. Happiness brings clarity.

Everything becomes more vivid…

the sky is bluer, the grass greener,

ideas more abundant.

When we're happy and having fun,

we simply become better.

Better parents, better lovers,

better friends, and better leaders.

We become better everything

when we're happy and having fun.

Positive attitudes breed collaboration.

Humans have a fundamental

need to express, contribute

and be heard.

Without the ability to express

we are silenced prisoners

chained to a cold dark void.

Unlock your own inhibitions

and stoicism. Feel.

Feelings are powerful.

Just don't become a slave to them.

The objective is to feel

something, acknowledge

the emotion,

leverage the emotion by acting,

then let them go.

CHAPTER 21

HOMEWARD BOUND

Less than 60 minutes remained

before the premiere of *Mystère*.

"That's a wrap everybody!"

Louis, the French-Canadian

stage manager yelled with a hint of panic.

"You must be in the Green Room

in ten minutes.

No excuses!"

A nervous buzz conjugated our

discussions as the final

rehearsal ended.

We dispersed.

Surely, they're going to cancel the show!

How can you perform a show

you've never performed before?

One performer's creativity,

had triggered the creativity

of an intense and passionate director.

The director's courage to pivot

on a dime at the 11th hour

put in motion

one of the most spectacular

watershed moments

I'd ever perceived and

might ever witness.

One moment of complete

surrender to the power of the

imagination, and trusting

creative instincts, gave birth

to something different,

unique and magnificent.

Vegas entertainment,

if not world entertainment

history was made.

The tension-filled, claustrophobic

Green Room lacked oxygen.

Franco Dragone and Cirque's VP,

Gilles St. Croix addressed us

with extreme urgency to

reveal our dramatic fate.

They drew up the last ten

minutes of Mystère with

dry erasers on the board

like a coach would a sports play.

A barrage of questions,

concerns, and suggestions

ricochet from the board,

ceiling, walls, and stressed

faces of the cast. Gilles,

Franco and Louis too

appeared anxious.

I was in awe of this collectively

open-minded approach to

fixing a problem by

focusing on the solution.

We headed to our respective

dressing rooms to prepare for battle.

Let's do this!

"Stand by five minutes.

Attention, cinq minutes, vnimaniye pyat minut,"

declared Louis over the PA

system in English, French and Russian.

The three languages were commonly

used during all announcements

to accommodate the dominant

languages spoken by the cast.

I'd never felt so much anticipation,

excitement and trepidation all at once.

My inner child's curiosity

couldn't help by spy the audience

before the show from the tech ring.

Not a seat available.

ShowTime!

The show ran smoothly until

we reached the final ten,

un-choreographed minutes.

What was on the board again?

Am I supposed to be on this

side or the other side?

Stage managers consulted

their hand-written notes.

They directed us to our places

with a hint of uncertainty.

"Aren't we supposed to be —"

"Hmm…"

We made it through to the

end of the show!

The cast ran forward and

filled the edge of the circular stage.

We struck our final pose and

signature salute of *Mystère*—

a powerful and poetic grasp

of thin air with our hands in

front and above our heads,

ending in a clenched fist

metaphorically seizing the moment

with pride and joy.

Standing ovation.

Black out!

But now came a reprise.

An element of disaster

loomed on the horizon.

When the lights came back

on and the music started up

again, we'd create two lines,

splitting stage left and stage right,

and run to the front and center of

the stage to acknowledge the

audience one last time

before exiting the stage.

As performers rushed in a chaotic

manner to wave goodbye to the audience,

the stilt characters weren't

sure what to do.

Through the commotion,

the two tallest stilts, walking on

twelve feet of metal piping with only

a peg to balance on, tripped

over the running performers.

From my six-foot stilts,

I watched them fall in

slow motion as they desperately

tried to keep their balance.

Their long fall, approximately

eighteen feet from head to "toe,"

took forever.

Their distorted, stick- figure

bodies finally slammed into the stage.

Both were briefly motionless.

Performers jumped over the silent

characters to honor the plan of the reprise.

I stayed, watching in disbelief and anger.

How could they be so preoccupied

with a bow and ignore their friends?

The show must go on, I guess.

The music ended, and the stage

went black to signify the end.

I heard only painful groans from

my fallen colleagues.

This was not a part of the drawn-up plan!

Paramedics waited outside

in the event of a major injury.

Would this be their first call to action?

CHAPTER 22

FAILURE

Michael Jordan once said,

"I've missed over nine-thousand

shots in my career.

I've lost over three-hundred games.

Twenty-six times,

I've been trusted to take

the game winning shot and missed.

I've failed over and over

again in my life, and

that is why I succeed."

To optimize one's

creative potential, the starting

point must be a mentality

of open-mindedness where

everything and anything is possible,

knowing failure is probable,

if not a must.

You can't be afraid to fail.

In fact, failure is your friend. Unless

you fail due to negligence or not caring, which could

compromise and dilute your product or service… your

business and personal brand reputation.

CHAPTER 23

BUMPY

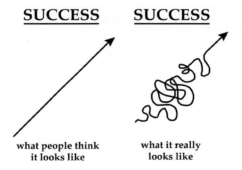

SUCCESS   SUCCESS

what people think
it looks like

what it really
looks like

In the beginning of their journey,

Cirque du Soleil faced the wrath

of skeptics and critics.

They were accused of violating,

if not raping the age-old tradition of circus.

No animals?

No ring?

Upscale theatrical expression?

What a joke they called them!

Growth and transformation always

come with the risk of alienation,

resistance or failure.

It's a delicate dance.

If you have enough passion,

enough patience and perseverance,

and enough resources, (time and money)

the journey becomes easier.

Not all creatives and artists

are celebrated.

Some fade into the abyss

shrouded by humiliation,

shame and insignificance.

Take that risk and express yourself.

Invite those in your tribe to do the same.

Creativity and open-mindedness

are contagious. Cirque's

culture and approach infected me.

Watching and experiencing this company

think like an artist changed my life.

Life is all about change.

Embrace it well.

Please, keep that precious and

powerful mind of yours open...

you never know.

Enjoy the ride even

when it's bumpy.

Step back, look at the canvas from

a different perspective.

The answers are always there.

CHAPTER 24

TIME

The theatre house lights came on.

My fallen stilt friends showed

signs they had survived.

Cirque, we made it!

Within a few weeks of the premiere,

Time Magazine shared an

article regarding entertainment.

Mystère had been listed as one

of the top five best shows in the world.

BRAVO!

Not bad for a bunch of

street-performers from Montreal

who didn't listen to naysayers

and doubters.

Don't you dare listen to

naysayers and doubters.

Don't you dare listen to

that voice in your head either…

you know, the one that is saying,

you're not good enough,

or your idea won't work.

It may not work the first time.

Many of my canvases have been disasters.

I let the paint dry, "cry"…

and go again when needed.

Regardless of this initial triumph

of Cirque du Soleil, *Mystère*

was still an infant.

All Cirque shows need time

to mature, like a fine wine.

The first six months of any

Cirque production is really about

eliminating the kinks and

polishing the finish until it

shines memorably.

Even after the incredible shine

has been achieved, growth,

exploration, improvement,

and change remain on the agenda.

In modern Japanese business philosophy

this is referred to as KAIZEN **(1986 Masaaki Imai).**

It means, ongoing or continuous improvement.

THIRTY YEARS LATER

My Cirque career ended prematurely and dramatically.

The lessons learned during my five amazing

years and over 2,000 plus shows in this bold

and daring company taught me so much

about life: courage, risk-taking and pushing

beyond that which we know, and that which

we feel safe with were priceless.

I became a different human-being.

As I write this book, regularly entering my

art studio for inspiration because I feel stuck,

broken, hopeful, afraid, fulfilled, hurt, confused,

yet eager to live out loud,

I remind myself, to just BE.

Be me. Be free.

Be authentic. Be bold… be brave.

Be the artist.

The artist that learned to fly,

flip, twist and fail spectacularly in a

zany French-Canadian circus.

I became much more INTENTIONAL

with my creativity. It gave me wings.

It empowered me to reach higher...

CLOSING THOUGHT

Growth is a never-ending

process that requires risk,

courage, and a childlike spirit

that wants to play in the sand

and build sandcastles that

haven't yet been imagined.

Failure will be a part of that

fascinating journey.

The key to failing is to fail quickly.

Bon voyage et bonne chance ...

safe and happy travels and good luck

as you pursue the new, the different,

and the original.

Dare to dream.

Dare to risk.

Dare to fall off the edge and make a

spectacular fool of yourself.

Dare to be different and innovate.

Where you go from here is up to you.

Dare to create your own

masterpiece, on your own terms,

with YOUR authentic voice.

You are now free to spread

your wings fly beyond the

net into whatever future

your imagination and inner

artist creates.

BRAVO!

CREATIVITY IS CONTAGIOUS.

PASS IT ON.

ALBERT EINSTEIN

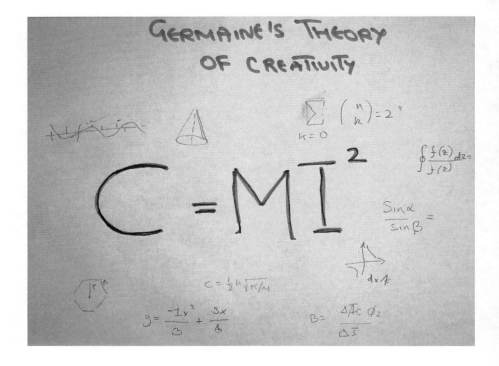

Creativity equals Mindset
multiplied by Imagination
to the power of 2.

PS. If you enjoyed this book, please leave a review on Amazon and recommend to your friends. If you didn't enjoy this book, please recommend to your enemies.

About the Author

 Since leaving Cirque du Soleil, Vital Germaine started an entertainment production company that produced live events around the world. Many years later, following a newfound sense of purpose and passion, he started a consulting company called ENGAGEteams360.

Vital has become a reputable, dynamic, and engaging public speaker, corporate trainer, and transformation leader.

Vital delivers relevant, impactful, and transformational workshops, keynotes and trainings that inspire meaningful transformation.

For more information on Vital's books, products, and services log on to: VitalGermaine.com.

If you enjoyed the read, please leave a review on Amazon and share the book with a friend, colleague or organization.

Thank you.

Other books by Vital

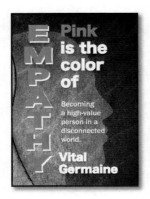

PINK IS THE COLOR OF EMPATHY is partially about life in the amazing Cirque du Soleil. It is more a touching story filled with hope and belief. An inspirational story that defines the power of the human spirit. A spirit we all have.

This book is about becoming a high-value person. Empathy is the superpower to help you become that.

Empathy, when used as a tool of love and understanding, strengthens all relationships, inspiring deep and meaningful connections that elevate the spirits of others... and your own. We all want empathy when it's our turn, but many of us lack the ability to share it with others.

The tools in this book will help you become a high-value person within your family, circle of friends, community and at work.

Other books by Vital

3 SIMPLE STEPS is a short - childlike story written for adults who are on a journey of growth and healing. Be inspired. Feel compelled to overcome and reach higher. Follow the journey of a young student whose future is forever changed when a teacher reveals the magic and wisdom of a journal an elder once shared.

A charming coffee table book for a rainy day when the desire to design a better life becomes apparent.

- BRAVO
- ENJOY BEING INSPIRED
- IT REALLY GOT MY ATTENTION
- SUPER FUN LITTLE BOOK
- YOU'll READ IT OVER AND OVER AGAIN

Other books by Vital

FLYING WITHOUT A NET is partially about life in the amazing Cirque du Soleil. It is more a touching story filled with hope and belief. An inspirational story that defines the power of the human spirit. A spirit we all have.

The top-selling book has been called:

- o INSPIRATIONAL
- o A MUST READ.
- o STUNNING MEMOIR
- o COULDN'T PUT IT DOWN
- o BEST READ OF THE YEAR
- o READ COVER TO COVER IN ONE SITTING

Other books by Vital

FLYING WITHOUT A NET 2.0 is the sequel to FLYING WITHOUT A NET. If you are looking to overcome professional and personal challenges, soar and achieve more in life, then this book is for you.

It's been called:

- A 10!
- CAPTIVATING. COMPELLING!
- EXTRAORDINARY!
- TRIUMPHANT. FIVE STARS!
- DIDN'T WANT IT TO END!
- WONDERFUL MUST READ
- POWERFUL, INSPIRATIONAL
- MUST READ. VERY INSPIRING
- VITAL DID IT AGAIN!

Other books by Vital

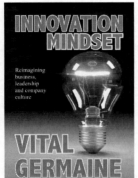

INNOVATION MINDSET is the extended business version of this book. It's designed for entrepreneurs, business owners, executives, leaders and cultures to be inspired and enabled to navigate change. It includes a series of action steps to simplify transformation.

The book includes interviews with thought leaders from different industries: Tim Sanders, New York Times Best-selling author and former Yahoo executive.

Jordan Adler, Best-selling author and MLM Millionaire. Randy Sutton, former police detective and TV News contributor. Dennis Bonilla, former U.S. Navy Nuke!

It's been called:

- o Brilliant!
- o A must-have for your leadership library!
- o Calling all leaders. I highly recommend this book.
- o Interesting and entertaining, genius and genuine.
- o Definitely the inspiration I needed to venture outside my comfort zone and CREATE!
- o Great stories and illustrations of relevant and timely principles any leader, in any organization can apply to take their life and career to new heights.

Other books by Vital

REACHING HIGHER, 21 Ways To Keep Life Positive, is a quick and easy read to help lift your spirits on those slower days when you need more than a strong coffee to get you going.

It's been called:

- Highly beneficial for everyone.
- A beautiful collection of mindset reminders.
- Get this NOW!
- Uplifted and encouraged
- Inspiring

VitalGermaine.com
THE INSPIRATIONALIST

@VitalGermaine

Made in United States
North Haven, CT
04 January 2025

63859098R00126